TAKE ACTION

SAVE LIFE ON EARTH

SAVE BIRDS

Stephanie Feldstein

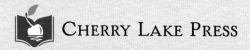

Published in the United States of America by Cherry Lake Publishing Group
Ann Arbor, Michigan
www.cherrylakepublishing.com

Reading Adviser: Beth Walker Gambro, MS, Ed., Reading Consultant, Yorkville, IL
Book Designer: Felicia Macheske

Photo Credits: © FotoRequest/Shutterstock, cover; © Eric Isselee/Shutterstock, 5; © Wang LiQiang/Shutterstock, 5, back cover; © Kurtis Sutley/Shutterstock, 9; Library of Congress, W. M. Morrison photographer, Lillian Russell,-1922, LOC Control No: 2005687508, 11; Library of Congress, Carol M Highsmith, photographer. Andrew De Luna, dancer at the Celebrations of Traditions Pow Wow, San Antonio in Texas, 2014., LOC Control No. 2014632457, 13; OMG_Studio/Shutterstock, 14; Khairil Azhar Junos/Shutterstock, 17; © Pocket Canyon Photography/Shutterstock; © Stephanie Foote, 21; © Rob McKay/Shutterstock, 23; © Ranglen/Shutterstock, 24; © kimberrywood/Shutterstock, 27; © Manop Boonpeng/Shutterstock, 31, © David Jeffrey Ringer/Shutterstock, back cover

Graphics © Pavel K; © Panimoni/Shutterstock; © Hulinska Yevheniia/Shutterstock; © Vector Place/Shutterstock; © Happy Art/Shutterstock; © Ihnatovich Maryia/Shutterstock; © Eugenia Petrovskaya/Shutterstock; © graficriver_icons_logo/Shutterstock

Copyright © 2024 by Cherry Lake Publishing Group

All rights reserved. No part of this book may be reproduced or utilized in any form or by any means without written permission from the publisher.

Cherry Lake Press is an imprint of Cherry Lake Publishing Group.

Library of Congress Cataloging-in-Publication Data has been filed and is available at catalog.loc.gov.

Cherry Lake Publishing Group would like to acknowledge the work of the Partnership for 21st Century Learning, a Network of Battelle for Kids. Please visit *http://www.battelleforkids.org/networks/p21* for more information.

Printed in the United States of America
Corporate Graphics

Note from publisher: Websites change regularly, and their future contents are outside of our control. Supervise children when conducting any recommended online searches for extended learning opportunities.

Table of Contents

INTRODUCTION

Birds and the Extinction Crisis

Bee hummingbirds are the smallest birds in the world. They weigh less than a penny. Ostriches are the biggest. They can grow up to 9 feet (2.7 meters) tall. Birds come in many sizes, shapes, and colors. Some, like ostriches, can't fly. But they all have feathers, wings, and beaks. They lay eggs. Amazingly, they're closely related to dinosaurs.

Birds are found across the planet. They live in hot deserts and freezing arctic lands. They're found in forests and prairies. **Habitat** is the place where wild animals live. But bird habitats are being replaced by cities, farms, and roads. They're being destroyed by **climate change**.

Extinction is when all of one kind of plant or animal dies. It affects wild plants and animals. An extinct plant or animal is gone forever. Scientists say we're in an extinction **crisis**. When wildlife goes extinct, it weakens **ecosystems**. Healthy ecosystems provide food, shelter, water, and clean air. Life on Earth needs all kinds of plants and animals.

Nearly 11,000 different kinds of birds live on Earth. At least 1,400 of them are threatened with extinction. Many more are shrinking in number. They need a safe place to nest. They need places to rest when they fly long distances. They need protection from **toxic** chemicals.

We can stop the extinction crisis. People like us need to take action. Governments and businesses need to act, too. By working together, we can save birds.

Why We Need
BIRDS

Birds are a big part of human culture. People love watching birds and listening to their songs. Birds are in our stories, art, and traditions.

Birds are important to ecosystems in many ways. Many eat insects and rodents. This helps protect crops. It stops the spread of disease. It keeps ecosystems in balance. Some birds, like vultures, eat dead animals. They clean up carcasses before they can rot. Other birds drink nectar from flowers. The powder from the flowers, called pollen, sticks to their beaks. They carry it to other flowers where it helps make new seeds. This is called **pollination**. Flowering plants and trees need pollination to grow.

Lots of birds eat berries. They fly around and poop out the seeds. This spreads the seeds so new plants can grow. Bird poop also works like fertilizer. It helps make soil healthy. It keeps ecosystems growing. The new plants feed and shelter other animals.

Birds are so important that scientists look to them to see if an ecosystem is healthy. If birds are healthy, it's a good sign for the other plants and animals. If they're not, the whole ecosystem could be in trouble.

CHAPTER ONE

Flying into Danger

Humans create dangers that birds can't fly away from. The biggest threat is habitat loss. Birds need safe places to nest and find food. The growth of farms and towns is destroying much bird habitat.

Some birds learn to live alongside people. They build nests on buildings. They become part of the urban ecosystem. But this has dangers of its own. Birds get hit by cars. They mistake trash for food. They're exposed to toxic chemicals.

Between 20 and 50 percent of all kinds of birds are **migratory**. They travel between different habitats. They often fly from summer homes to warmer places in the winter. Migratory birds need rest stops along their journey. They need safe paths to fly. Between 365 and 988 million birds die each year crashing into buildings.

This is a flock of sandhill cranes in New Mexico. Many sandhill cranes migrate to (and pass through) New Mexico during winter months.

TURNING POINT

In the early 1900s, wealthy women wore hats with feathers. The feathers came from all sorts of birds. Some hats even had entire dead birds on them. Tens of millions of birds were killed for hats. People collected exotic bird feathers and skins. Fashion was driving birds to extinction.

People realized that fashion wasn't worth losing birds forever. Some women protested feather hats. They started new feather-free trends. They taught people to enjoy birds in nature. Organizations formed to protect birds.

The U.S. government passed the Migratory Bird Treaty Act in 1918. Migratory birds were hurt the most by the feather trade. The new law protected them. People couldn't sell feathers. They couldn't even keep feathers they found. This helped stop people from harming wild birds to collect or sell their feathers. It saved countless birds from extinction. It inspired other wildlife protection laws for decades.

American Actress Lillian Russell (1861–1922) wearing a hat decorated with feathers

Farming causes a lot of habitat loss. Forests and prairies are turned into fields to grow crops. Most of those fields are sprayed with **pesticides**. Pesticides are chemicals made to kill things like weeds or bugs. But they also kill important wildlife like birds.

Climate change is altering bird habitats. Many ecosystems are getting too warm. Food isn't always available when birds need it. Some birds are moving to cooler places. But birds living high in the mountains have nowhere cooler to go. Sea levels are also rising. Beaches are disappearing. There's less room for birds that nest in the sand.

The Migratory Bird Treaty Act stopped people from collecting feathers. But it didn't consider Indigenous cultures. Feathers have spiritual meaning in these cultures. Many Indigenous tribes use them in ceremonies. They're passed down to children. They're given as gifts.

The law said people had to prove where their feathers came from. Tribes couldn't always do that. That made it harder for them to practice their religion. The law harmed Indigenous culture. In 1962, the law was updated so tribes could collect and use feathers.

Invasive species are plants or animals that don't belong in an ecosystem. They harm native wildlife. Climate change often causes invasive species to move into new ecosystems. In Hawaii, the warmer weather brings more mosquitoes. They carry deadly diseases. These diseases may make native birds extinct.

Humans also introduce invasive species. House cats that roam outdoors are an invasive species. Outdoor cats kill between 1.3 and 4 billion birds every year in the United States

◄ Red imported fire ants are an invasive species in the United States. They harm ground-nesting birds by eating their eggs and nestlings.

CHAPTER TWO

Be a Bird-Friendly Neighbor

People have many ways to be better neighbors to birds. You can start by making your yard bird-friendly. Grow **native plants**. These are plants that occur naturally in your area. They'll provide the best food and shelter for local birds. You don't need a big yard. Even native plants in outdoor pots or a courtyard can provide a snack.

Let your yard or garden get a little messy. Leaves and sticks help the soil stay healthy, which brings more bugs for birds to eat. Birds use yard debris to make nests. But make sure you clean up any trash. It can be deadly for birds. Some will take bits of plastic, ribbon, and other litter to their nests. Others might eat it. Then they can't digest their food.

A healthy garden can provide food to birds, like this American goldfinch.

Outdoor cats kill more birds than any other single threat from humans. House cats don't belong in the wild. They belong in your home. You can protect birds by keeping your cat indoors. It's safer for your cat, too.

There are many ways to keep indoor cats happy. Toys let them play at hunting. Some people build screened-in areas for their cats. These are called catios. These areas let cats enjoy the outdoors without hurting wildlife.

Don't use pesticides on your plants or around your house. Pesticides poison birds. They kill the bugs birds like to eat. Chemicals that poison mice and rats also kill birds. Hawks, eagles, and owls eat the poisoned animals and get sick. Bird feeders can be a great way to provide food for birds. It's also fun to watch and learn about birds that visit your feeder. Different birds have different tastes. Think about what kind of birds you want to visit your yard. Research the best kind of feeder and food for those birds. Clean your feeder every couple of weeks. This helps protect birds from disease.

Birds fly into windows because the reflection looks like the sky to them. Breaking up the reflection helps them notice the glass. Window decals help protect birds. Bird stores sell decals. You can also use holiday window decorations or look online for how to make your own.

Birds use the stars and moon to find their way in the dark. Bright lights confuse them. Turning off lights at night helps protect migrating birds.

CONSERVATION CHAMPION

David Lindo grew up in London, England. But that didn't stop him from finding nature in the city. He watched birds in his backyard and in local parks. He realized nature was all around him.

Birds taught Lindo not to be afraid of being different. They helped him find strength. They helped him connect with the bigger world. They taught him to love. That's the lesson Lindo shares with others.

Lindo didn't know much about how to identify birds when he was a kid. What mattered was that he noticed them. He encourages people to look up, watch, and listen. He tells people to see the city as birds see it. Then people can later research what they experience.

Today Lindo is known as the Urban Birder. He travels all over the world. He helps people in cities look at birds in new ways. Everyone can enjoy birds. It doesn't matter where you are or who you are. He works to make sure diverse people feel welcome in the outdoors.

Lindo's lessons help people understand how their actions affect wildlife. He connects people to nature. That love of nature helps save birds.

CHAPTER THREE

Technology in Action

Most of the best ways to protect birds are very low-tech. Protecting forests, prairies, and wetlands helps save bird habitats. **Organic** food is grown without toxic chemicals. Buying organic food helps protect birds. And using less plastic is the best way to keep it out of the environment.

But new technology is also helping save birds. **Fossil fuels** are a major cause of climate change. Switching to **renewable energy** will help slow climate change. Renewable energy is power from the sun or wind. Solar panels on existing structures are the most wildlife-friendly choice. They don't create new development in bird habitats. They don't cause new hazards to migratory birds. Researchers are finding new ways to add solar power to buildings. They're making it easier and cheaper. They're figuring out how to capture solar energy from roads and windows.

The habitat of the snowy owl is threatened by climate change. Renewable energy can help these birds survive.

Renewable energy is an important part of saving birds. But it can create new hazards. Sometimes birds fly into wind turbines. They can be harmed by large solar farms. Renewable energy sources must be built in ways that protect birds. They should be put in places that aren't migratory routes. They shouldn't disrupt bird habitats.

However, far more birds are killed by fossil fuels than wind or solar farms. Many more are threatened by climate change. Careful planning of renewable energy sources helps both the climate and the birds.

Technology is also used to study birds in the wild. Researchers attach tiny tracking devices called **geolocators** to birds. These devices are so small and light that birds hardly notice them. Geolocators track where the birds go. They record **migration** patterns. They help identify threats. This helps scientists know where to focus **conservation** efforts. Conservation is action to protect wildlife and nature.

Digital cameras help scientists observe birds in the wild. They don't have to disturb the birds once the camera is set up. They can study the birds from afar. They can watch the birds' natural behavior. They can see how they raise their young in nests. They can count how many different birds visit a habitat. The more scientists learn about birds, the better they can protect them.

SPEAK UP FOR BIRDS

Renewable energy can help protect birds from your backyard to Antarctica. But it's not easy for people to switch to renewable energy on their own. Laws can make it hard to put solar panels on houses. Most cars still run on gas. There aren't enough charging stations for electric vehicles. That's where your local government officials can help. They can pass laws to make it easier for people to get solar power. They can put solar panels on government buildings. They can replace gas-powered government vehicles with electric ones. They can add more charging stations.

Write a letter to your mayor or town council. Tell them why birds are important. Tell them how climate change is harming birds. Ask them to make renewable energy available to everyone. Ask them to use renewable energy on city property.

Writing a letter to your city's mayor or town council is one way you can speak up for birds.

Many towns have a **Climate Action Plan. The plan says how the town will fight climate change. Most plans have goals for renewable energy. They can also have steps to protect wildlife. Ask your local leaders to make sure their plan protects birds.**

CREATE A BACKYARD BIRD COUNT

Scientists say that watching birds makes people happier. But it's also a fun way to help scientists protect birds. Sharing the birds you see helps scientists monitor them. If you're new to bird-watching, here's how to get started:

1 Start looking for birds every time you're outside. Notice where you see them. Try to spot differences between birds.

2 Research the birds in your area. Create a checklist of birds you want to see. Add descriptions to help you identify them.

3 Practice watching birds. You'll keep getting better at knowing where to look for them. You'll learn how to identify them.

Now that you're a birder, start tracking the birds you see. Use your checklist to record which birds you find. Apps can help you learn to identify birds. The eBird app helps you organize your bird list. It shares your observations with scientists. The Merlin Bird ID app helps identify birds. It uses sound, size, color, and habitat to tell you what kind of bird you're watching.

Bird counts are when lots of people watch birds over the same time period. This gives scientists a snapshot of how birds are doing around the world. The Christmas Bird Count happens every winter. Communities organize groups to go out and count birds together. The Great Backyard Bird Count happens every February. For 4 days, people count as many birds as they can. Then they report what kinds they saw and how many. Find out how to join by having an adult help you search "Great Backyard Bird Count" on the internet.

Bird counts are a great way to learn more about birds. You can find other bird lovers in your community. You can help scientists save birds.

You can watch birds almost anywhere, including your own yard or a nearby park.

LEARN MORE

Gray, Susan H. *Whooping Crane*. Ann Arbor, MI: Cherry Lake Publishing, 2008.

Nussbaum, Ben. *Saving Migratory Birds*. Huntington Beach, CA: Teacher Created Materials Publishing, 2019.

Zambello, Erika. *Backyard Birding for Kids*. Cambridge, MN: Adventure Publications, 2022.

GLOSSARY

climate change (KLY-muht CHAYNJ) changes in weather, temperatures, and other natural conditions over time

conservation (kahn-suhr-VAY-shuhn) action to protect wildlife and nature

crisis (KRY-suhss) a very difficult time or emergency

ecosystems (EE-koh-sih-stuhmz) places where plants, animals, and the environment rely on each other

extinction (ik-STINK-shuhn) when all of one kind of plant or animal die

fossil fuels (FAH-suhl FYOO-uhls) fuels like oil, gas, and coal that come from the remains of plants and animals and are burned for energy

geolocators (gee-oh-LOH-kay-tuhrz) electronic devices that track location

habitat (hah-BUH-tat) the natural home of plants and animals

invasive species (in-VAY-siv spee-SHEEZ) plants or animals that don't belong in an ecosystem

migration (my-GRAY-shuhn) a journey to a new or seasonal home

migratory (MY-gruh-tohr-ee) describing animals that travel between habitats

native plants (NAY-tiv PLANTZ) plants that are a natural part of an ecosystem

organic (or-GAH-nik) food or other plants grown without toxic chemicals

pesticides (PEH-stuh-sydes) toxic chemicals made to kill a plant or animal that might harm crops

pollination (pah-luh-NAY-shuhn) moving pollen between flowers to help plants make new seeds

renewable energy (rih-NOO-uh-buhl EH-nuhr-jee) energy that comes from sources nature will replace; this energy does not pollute air or water

toxic (TAK-sik) something that is harmful or poisonous

INDEX